PUGS

Complete Pugs Information, The Ultimate Guide To Pugs Care, Feeding, Housing, Training

Harmann Blanda

Table of Contents

CHAPTER ONE

PUGS

Pugs are sturdy and easy to care for, but it is important to note that they do not do well in hot, humid weather and must be closely monitored for heatstroke.

Pug To sum up quickly

Care must be taken to prevent dryness around the Pug's prominent eyes.

They are between 10 and 11 inches tall and 14 and 18 pounds (six to eight kilograms). They have sturdy bodies and a square shape. As befits their mastiff ancestry, pugs are the hardiest of the toy dog breeds.

Pugs have large, round heads that are distinguished by their short muzzles and deep forehead wrinkles. Those who have a vertical crease in their forehead are often referred to as having a "prince mark" because it supposedly looks like the Chinese character for "prince."

Because of how far out they stick, the eyes are more likely to be injured. Tightly coiled around the hip, the tail.

Short and dense, their double coat is extremely thick. Apt, fawn, silver, and even black are among the possible hues. All dogs, with the exception of black ones, have a dark muzzle and ears, and some even have a darker back. A black velvety texture can be found in the ear canal.

Pugs are not as outgoing as other toy dog breeds. Their sense of humor is more sardonic and serious. Plenty of dog in a small package, as the breed's motto, "multum in parvo," suggests. While pugs have a reputation for being obstinate, in most cases they genuinely enjoy pleasing their owners.

It's rare to see excessive barking, digging, or chewing from one of these dogs. Pugs get along well with other dogs and are sturdy enough to be around kids. They enjoy being around people and can be affectionate when they do. In line with their classification, they make excellent housemates.

As a result of:

Pugs are very low maintenance, but they can easily gain weight if their diet and exercise aren't closely monitored. Due to their short muzzles, they are particularly vulnerable to heatstroke in hot and humid climates. Because of their short muzzles, pugs often snore. The large, vulnerable eyes require special care to prevent drying out. Pugs have long lifespans, typically between 14 and 15 years.

Exercising your pug daily is the best way to combat their chubbiness. While they may have sounded a heroic alarm in the past, these friendly canines are more likely to wag their tails at visitors than to keep anyone safe. Pugs benefit from being exposed to other animals and humans, so socialization is important for maintaining their friendly nature.

Maintaining a clean appearance in the facial wrinkles and shedding the dense coat both necessitate regular grooming. Daily maintenance typically consists of a quick brush through with a hound mitt and a wet washcloth over the face and ears.

History:

The pug may have been bred down from a local mastiff-type dog in China, but despite its reputation for having originated in Holland, the pug actually originated in Asia. The Dutch East India Company used their trading ships to bring the little dogs with the round heads and wrinkled expressions to Holland. Pugs have been associated with the House of Orange since 1572, when one of the breed's members sounded the alarm that saved Prince William from an oncoming Spanish army.

The duke and duchess of Windsor had a pug, and Napoleon's wife also kept one as a pet. Many pugs can be seen in paintings from Victorian England, when they became the dog breed of choice.

Some have speculated that the name "pug" was originally derived from the Latin word for fist, "pugnus." This would account for the dog's characteristically round face and skull. The dogs' primary purpose in life, and contrary to their name, is to be companions, rather than guards.

Pugs have adorable squishy faces and personalities to match. This breed is great for laid-back households and people who like to dote on their pets because of its mischievous nature, but it is still loved by its owners. In spite of this, pugs share many of the same health problems as other dogs. Everything you need to know about taking care of a pug in your home is right here.

Pugs, which were originally developed as lap dogs, require constant human company and are happiest when they are in close proximity to their owners. Pugs have a reputation for being the canine version of the class clown due to their goofy antics and rambunctious nature. They think that the fact that they are breathing your air is enough to make you happy.

Pugs, with their calm demeanor and friendly nature, make great family pets. They shed so much, though, that you'll need a good vacuum. Pugs are playful but don't need a lot of exercise, so they can sit around and watch TV or go for a walk with their owner if that's what they prefer. Even though they can be stubborn and independent thinkers, pugs make wonderful pets and loyal companions.

Pugs are adorable, but before bringing one home, prospective owners should learn about the health issues associated with the brachycephalic breed.

Pugs are a historic dog breed with a long history of royal patronage, including with Chinese emperors, Josephine Bonaparte, and Queen Victoria.

CHAPTER TWO

Appearance

As a small dog that packs a lot of muscle onto its square frame (despite weighing only 14-18 pounds, as reported by the American Kennel Club), the pug has been given the motto "multum in parvo" (a lot in a little). Pugs are typically either fawn with a black mask or all black, though there are some tonal variations within these two basic colors. The range of a fawn or tan coat's color is wide, from a warm apricot to a cool, infrequently seen silver. Their short, flat, black muzzles are etched with deep wrinkles, making them instantly recognizable. Their large, expressive eyes take up most of their jovial, wrinkled face and can convey anything from surprise and happiness to curiosity and even anger. It's common for them to have moles on their cheeks (which they call "beauty spots") and a distinct "thumb mark" on their forehead.

Although it appears short, their coat is actually double-layered, and they shed heavily year-round but especially in the summer. Nichols warns, "I'd call them monster shedders," so be ready to have your clothes completely covered in fur. The AKC specifies that a pug must have a double curl in its tail.

Smooshed-faced dogs, or brachycephalic dogs, like pugs, face some unique difficulties due to their genetic make-up. One of these is that they may have tongues that are physically too big for their mouths, so they are always making a goofy face.

Temperament

A pug's ideal location is at your side. Having been selected for companionship, they have no qualms about spending the night curled up next to you in bed. On the other hand, fair warning: You might want to get some earplugs if you live with a pug because they wheeze, snort, and snore a lot. If you don't show them lots of love and attention, or if you leave them alone for long periods of time, they will be very unhappy and will let you know about it.

A pug is not suited for tasks such as hunting, guarding, or retrieving. A pug would never engage in such behavior. However, the PDCA notes that this does not mean pugs aren't game for some lighthearted fun and games. Pugs are witty little dogs that can come up with their own amusing antics, but you should really pay attention to the show they're putting on for your own good.

Left: Pugs were designed to be man's best friend, and they take that role very seriously. They

are adored by anyone under the age of eighteen due to their gentle nature and childlike sense of humor.

The pug breed is known for its sensitivity to new environments and sounds. Assure them everything is going to be fine, and keep them close.

The Bare Essentials

Pugs are great with kids, and kids adore pugs. Even though pugs are small, they are more robust than other toy-sized dogs and eager to engage in play. Make sure the kids are aware that pugs aren't likely to play fetch or chase a soccer ball to prevent any disappointment. Pugs are generally friendly and sociable, and they get along well with other pets of all shapes and sizes.

Pugs are wonderful apartment pets and senior citizen companions because they don't need a lot of space to run around in. We're not implying that pugs are slothful just because they can sleep for up to 14 hours a day. Because it's hard for them to breathe, they don't bark very often, either. Short legs and difficulty breathing make them poor swimmers. When the weather is hot in the summer, they could use a refreshing swim in the pool, but they can't handle extreme temperatures. Left: Puggles, like most dogs, enjoy a good snoop around in the soil, but they aren't genetically predisposed to become hoarders. Be wary of their noses, though. That dirt has the potential to further congest their already congested airways.

Pugs have underbites, just like other brachycephalic breeds like shih tzus, bulldogs, and French bulldogs. However, you shouldn't automatically assume that you need to spend money on braces. Underbites are only fixed if they are painful or make chewing difficult, not because of how they look.

Right: The most common coat color combination for pugs is fawn and black, but black is the

only other recognized coat color for pugs. All-black pugs have coats that are completely devoid of any other color. In addition to the inevitable graying that comes with advancing age, that is.

CHAPTER THREE

Care

While your pug undoubtedly adores you, the PDCA warns that they may have an even deeper love for food. Because of their small size, they are prone to gaining weight quickly, so it is important to help manage their intake by limiting treats and not feeding them table scraps, no matter how cute and pleading they may look. It's also important to encourage exercise, even if it's not necessary every day. They come up with their own unique strategies to release excess energy.

In order to control excessive pug shedding, regular brushing (using a medium-bristle brush, a rubber grooming mitt, or a hound glove) and monthly bathing (about once a month) are recommended. And if they get wet and dirty, those cute wrinkles on your face can become a breeding ground for infection. In between baths, use a dry cotton ball to wipe your pug's wrinkles clean. The nails on a pug should be trimmed on a regular basis because they don't naturally wear down from being an outdoor dog. Pugs need to have their teeth brushed on a regular basis to prevent periodontal disease.

When it comes to training, Nichols says it can be difficult. These young people are more challenging to teach because they are not particularly interested in hearing your opinion. The use of harsh training methods should be avoided, as they are easily hurt.

Keep in mind that all they really want is to be with you.

Pugs' short muzzles make it hard for them to take deep breaths, so if you plan to sleep close to yours, you might want to invest in a pair of earplugs.

Health

In his article, Nichols warned that the first year of a pug's life can be quite pricey. "Their soft palates are often shortened surgically, and their noses are resected to make the nostrils larger. If these procedures are not done, your dog will snore loudly for the rest of its life."

Snoring aside, pugs' anatomy and physiology frequently get in the way of the dog's ability to breathe, work up a sweat, and stay cool when the temperature rises. These are all signs of brachycephalic obstructive airway syndrome (BOAS), which also manifests itself in problems with regurgitation, sleep, and abnormalities in the saliva.

Back problems, epilepsy, allergies, hemi-vertebrae (or misshapen vertebrae), hip dysplasia, patellar luxation, and nerve degeneration are just some of the other health issues that pugs can face. Pugs are susceptible to a wide range of skin conditions, such as yeast infections, staph infections, and demodectic mange.

In spite of the endearing appearance of their large, dark eyes, they are extremely defenseless. Pugs can suffer from a variety of eye problems, including corneal ulcers, proptosis, and dry eye. Your vet will need to treat skin conditions like walking dandruff, which is caused by a tiny mite. Obesity can make breathing difficulties worse in pugs, so it's important for owners to keep an eye on their pups' weight.

There are "many critical health-related welfare challenges to overcome for pugs," according to a 2022 study that compared pugs to other dogs. Three eye conditions were found to be more common in pugs than in the general population: BOAS, stenotic nares (narrow nostrils that make breathing difficult), and corneal ulceration. Instead, the study found that pugs had much lower adjusted odds of having heart murmurs or lipoma tumors.

Pug Dog Encephalitis is a fatal inflammatory brain disease that only affects pugs. Unfortunately, neither its cause nor a treatment are understood. A pug will convulse, spin in circles, go blind, and eventually go into a coma and die. The investigation continues at this time.

The pug is one of the oldest breeds of dog, and it has been featured in media for centuries. During the Victorian era, they enjoyed widespread acclaim, and you could regularly find depictions of them on postcards, in paintings, and even in figurine form.

The pug is a Chinese dog breed with a long history that may be the oldest of all dog breeds. The AKC claims that flat-faced, or short-nosed, toy dogs like the pug enjoyed a privileged status in China some two thousand years ago. Only those from outside of Asia received them as presents. However, Dutch merchants brought the breed to Europe in the 1500s and 1600s, where it quickly gained popularity among royal families.

Throughout their long history, various cultures have given this breed a variety of names, including lo-sze (in China), mopsi (in Finland), doguillo (in Spain), and mophonds (in the Netherlands). The AKC states that the name pug comes from the Latin word "pugnus," which means "fist," because of the resemblance between a pug's face and a clenched fist.

During the Victorian period, pugs were depicted frequently in art, including on postcards, paintings, and figurines. The aristocracy continued to keep them as pets for many years. In addition to Marie Antoinette's pug, Mops, Queen Victoria owned and bred a number of pugs. Early in the nineteenth century, they were standardized as a breed. In 1860, when the British took control of the Chinese Imperial Palace, they found several pugs there and began breeding them in England to improve the breed.

Pugs didn't arrive in the United States until after the Civil War. In 1885, the American Kennel Club officially recognized the breed. Pugs were once extremely popular, but interest in owning and breeding them began to wane around the 1930s, when the AKC officially recognized the Pug Dog Club of America as a legitimate organization.

On the left: Halloween costumes are a favorite among pug owners. At the 9th Annual Pug Parade on February 25, 2006 in Bradenton, Florida, this pug dressed as Yoda from the film Star Wars walks the runway.

Correct: Mushu, a trained pug, played the role of Frank the alien-like pug in the first two

Men in Black films. Los Angeles, California's Mann's Village and Bruin Theaters posed with him for the premiere of Men.

Random Information

According to the AKC, one legend states that the pug became the official dog of the Dutch royal family because one barked a warning that helped prevent the death of the Prince of Orange at the hands of invading Spanish troops.

The wrinkles on certain pugs, the story goes, were once highly prized in China because they resembled characters for good fortune in the local language.

A "grumble" is a term for a group of pugs.

To no one's surprise, adorable pug faces have been featured in Hollywood productions. Otis from Milo and Otis, Frank from Men in Black, and Percy from Pocahontas are all represented here. Many pugs have gained Internet fame in recent years.

Undoubtedly, Doug the Pug has the most devoted fanbase. The famous dog has more than 13 million followers on social media and is friends with celebrities like Joe Jonas and Shakira. There was a People's Choice Award for Animal Star given to Doug in 2019.

• Pug owners and fans are every bit as unique and endearing as their canine companions, often going so far as to dress up their canines for parties and parades.

THE END

* 9 7 9 8 3 5 8 6 1 4 0 6 2 *